A Guide to
ANCIENT CULTURES
of the Southwest

Mesa Southwest Museum — HOHOKAM NECKLACE

AN AMERICAN TRAVELER SERIES PUBLICATION

By Eleanor Ayer

© American Traveler Press. All rights reserved. This book or any parts thereof may not be reproduced in any manner whatsoever without written permission of the publisher:

2007 Printing

ISBN 13: 978-1-55838-126-1
ISBN 10: 1-55838-126-0

American Traveler Press
A Division of Primer Publishers
5738 North Central Avenue
Phoenix, Arizona 85012

1-800-521-9221

Cover photo Square Tower House at Mesa Verde N. P.
by Rich Hamilton

10 9 8 7 6 5 4

Printed in China. Published in the United States of America

WELCOME

Nearly two thousand years have passed since our southwestern ancestors inhabited the vast region now called the Colorado Plateau. They developed a superb irrigation system still in use today and apparently lived without war for hundreds of years. Indeed, we have much to learn from the prehistoric Indian cultures which first inhabited our American Southwest.

The Puebloans were predominate in today's Four Corners region, while other major cultures existed to the north and south. In Utah, the influence was strongly Fremont. Arizona was home to the Hohokam, Mogollon, Sinagua, Salado, and other prehistoric peoples. When the ancestral Puebloans left their homes in the north, many resettled in today's New Mexico. People living in modern-day pueblos like Acoma, Cochiti, Santa Clara, Taos and the Hopi Mesas of Arizona are their decendants.

These were prehistoric people. They had no written language and thus no way to record their history in print. But from the dwellings they built, the tools they designed, the pottery and baskets they constructed, and the clothes they fashioned, archeologists have been able to piece together glimpses into their way of life.

This material culture is both incredibly durable and extremely fragile. Fortunately many artifacts are protected in museums and government parks. But sadly we, travelers to this mystical past, are not sufficiently protective of our legacy. By federal law it is "illegal to excavate, remove, damage, alter or deface any archeological resources." Yet in spite of the law, damage occurs. It is our responsibility as travelers to these ancient sites to see that they are protected. Please, walk only in designated areas, touch no ruins, take nothing with you, and follow the rules.

You may wish to supplement your knowledge of the prehistoric Southwest with some of these references:

Easy Field Guide to Indian Art & Legends of the Southwest

Easy Field Guide to Rock Art Symbols of the Southwest

Easy Field Guide to Southwestern Petroglyphs

American Traveler—A Travelers Guide to Southwest Indian Arts & Crafts

American Traveler—Indians of Arizona A Guide to Arizona's Heritage

Our thanks to interpretive specialists at Mesa Verde National Park, the Mesa Southwest Museum, and many of the government sites mentioned in this book for their evaluations of the text.

Contents

The Southwest of the Ancients 4
The Early Basketmakers. 5
The Modified Basketmakers. 7
The Developmental Pueblo 8
The Neighbors. 9
The Classic Pueblo. 10
Salado and Classic Hohokam 11
The Pueblo IV Period 12
The Modern Pueblo 13
Mesa Verde National Park 14
Dinosaur National Monument 17
Hovenweep National Monument. 18
Canyonlands National Park 19
Capitol Reef National Park. 20
More Utah Sites. 21-23
Map 24-25
Glen Canyon National Recreation Area 26
Navajo National Monument 27
Canyon de Chelly National Monument 29
Grand Canyon National Park. 30
Wupatki & Sunset Crater. 31
Montezuma Castle & Tuzigoot. 32
Tonto National Monument 33
Casa Grande 34
More Arizona Sites. 35
Gila Cliff Dwellings 36
El Morro National Monument 37
Pecos National Historic Park. 38
Salinas Pueblo Missions 39
Bandelier National Monument 40
Chaco Culture National Historic Park 41
Aztec Ruins National Monument 44
Planning Your Travel. 45-48

J. Fleetman, Bureau of Reclamation   ESCALANTE RUINS

THE SOUTHWEST OF THE ANCIENTS

While Cleopatra was sitting on the throne of Egypt and Caesar was ruling Rome, ancient Indians were roaming the canyons and mesas of the American Southwest. On the walls of caves and cliffs they left drawings of birds, animals, and humans still visible today, a record of their lives in ancient times.

Over the millennia, a variety of different cultures inhabited this region. Paleo-Indians lived in the Southwest as early as 11,000 B.C. In caves in the Sandia Mountains of New Mexico, stone spear points have been found which date back even farther—some 25,000 years. Bones of bison, mammoths, and mastodons indicate that these early people hunted such big game.

Near Folsom, New Mexico, spear points were discovered with unique fluted or grooved tips and scraped surfaces. Their makers were Folsom Man who lived in the Southwest between 25,000 and 10,000 B.C. A similar culture, the Clovis people of New Mexico, had different but distinctive spear points. Stone artifacts are our only clues to these civilizations, for there was as yet no basketry, pottery, or metal. Another New Mexican people, the Cochise culture, inhabited the area for nearly 10,000 years, until 500 B.C.

The settlers whose evolution would lead to the Pueblo Culture first crossed a land bridge from Asia into Alaska about 12,000 years ago and followed the Rocky Mountain chain south. They were nomadic hunters and gatherers. Near Wendover, Utah, remains of their dwellings date to 9000 B.C. Archeologists call these groups who wandered the Colorado Plateau region Archaic people. Changes in the Archaic culture happened very slowly. It took several thousand years for the technique of raising corn to spread from southern cultures up north to what is now Colorado.

By 6000 B.C. there was less dependence on big game hunting, for the larger animals had migrated. People became more domestic. In their cliff dwelling homes they began weaving baskets and crafting sandals from native materials. Remains of these artifacts and primitive hunting tools have been found at many sites including Canyonlands National Park in Utah.

About the time of Christ, basket making began to proliferate. So dramatically did this craft alter the Archaic way of life that the people of the early A.D. years are known as Basketmakers. These early people are sometimes referred to as Anasazi; however, there never was an "Anasazi" tribe. Their culture would reach its peak more than a thousand years later during the Classic Pueblo period.

Mesa Verde N.P.   DIORAMA OF EARLY BASKETMAKERS SETTLEMENT

THE EARLY BASKETMAKERS

The high tableland of the Colorado Plateau, encompassing the Four Corners region of Colorado, Utah, Arizona, and New Mexico, is broadly referred to as the cradle of Pueblo civilization. Here, in the drainages of the San Juan, Little Colorado, Rio Grande, Gila and Salt Rivers, the Pueblo culture evolved about the time of Christ.

The earliest Puebloans were the Basketmakers, named for the products they wove from native apocynum (*uh-POSS-uh-num*) and yucca fibers. So skilled did the Basketmakers become at their craft that they wove baskets tight enough to hold water. There were baskets for gathering berries and nuts, baskets for cooking, even basket-type cradleboards for carrying infants. Weavers also crafted sandals from apocynum and yucca, and sometimes decorated them with buckskin.

The Early Basketmakers (1–500 A.D.), were short (5'3" men), brown-skinned people with thick black hair. Average lifespan was 35–40 years. They inhabited three major population centers where their artifacts can be seen today: the southern Colorado/Utah border area; Chaco Canyon, New Mexico; and Kayenta, Arizona.

The Early Basketmakers lived in alcoves or under overhanging cliffs. They were hunters and gatherers whose major big game weapon was an atlatl (*AT-lat-uhl*). The atlatl was a notched stick about two feet long which acted as an extension of the spearshaft. The hunter rested the end of his spear on the atlatl, thereby gaining distance and accuracy in his throw.

Greater hunting skills enabled the Basketmakers to spend less time hunting and more time at home. This increasingly sedentary lifestyle led to more permanent dwellings. The Basketmakers began building pithouses, so-called because a shelter of poles and adobe mud was built around and above a pit about 15 feet in diameter. Pithouse remains dating from 46 to 330 A.D. have been discovered near Durango, Colorado. They mark one of the earliest stages of pithouse use, but many later pithouses have also been found in the area.

On the fringes of the Pueblo territory lived other prehistoric Indian cultures. The Mogollon (*MUGGY-own*) occupied southeastern Arizona and west central New Mexico about 200 B.C. and flourished there until 1200 A.D. They were the first crafters of pottery in the Southwest, probably learning the skill from Indians in Mexico. By 700 A.D., the Mogollon had become so influenced by the Pueblo dwellers and other neighbors that it becomes difficult to distinguish their culture.

About the same time, along the Gila and Salt Rivers of Arizona, the Hohokam (*HO-ho-kawm*) culture developed. The major accomplishment of these people was a system of sophisticated irrigation canals reaching over 150 miles. In the Phoenix area, some of these canals were renovated and are still in use. Today's Tohono O'odham Indians of Arizona claim to be descendants of the Hohokam.

To the north and northwest of the Four Corners region, the Fremont culture was developing in Utah. This culture never became as highly developed as did the Puebloans, but they left behind an intriguing array of rock art. The Moab Rock Art Panel in Arches National Park is a Fremont legacy. Pottery shards, pictographs, and petroglyphs can be found at many Utah parks, including Capitol Reef, Fremont Indian State Park and Dinosaur National Monument on the Colorado border.

Over time, the pueblo dwellers learned to raise corn. Although their farm implements were little more than sharp sticks, farming gradually changed their way of life. It transformed them from a nomadic to a sedentary people. Living longer in one place made housing more important, bringing great changes in architecture. Basket making retained its importance, but in the coming age a new craft, potter, would further modify the Basketmakers' lives.

Mesa Southwest Museum   HOHOKAM CERAMIC FIGURE

THE MODIFIED BASKETMAKERS

This new age, 500–700 A.D., is known as the Modified Basketmaker Period. Pithouses proliferated as populations moved from cliffs to open areas where they built villages. On a mesa top in Chaco Canyon stands the remains of one village of 18 houses.

Ancestral farmers may have known how to raise beans for many years. But the women lacked a way to prepare them in a palatable manner. The modification that turned beans into a viable food was the crafting of pottery from clay. With clay pots, women could soak and bake directly over a fire rather than placing hot rocks in a basket of water to "cook" their food.

Pottery making was likely learned from their southern neighbors, the Hohokam and Mogollon. These people fired their pots in an oxygen-rich flame that produced a yellow, tan, or red finish. Fires on the mesa were lower in oxygen, and thus created gray pots. Using plant juices or mineral paste as dyes, craftsmen made black designs on gray or white backgrounds, a hallmark of Mesa Verdean pottery.

In the Modified Basketmaker age, the bow and arrow gradually replaced the atlatl, and full-grooved axes came into use. Sandal making reached its highest level of development. Cotton was added to the list of agricultural products. Religion became more influential, as the people began setting aside special areas of homes or villages for ceremonial events.

Pecos National Historic Park   KIVA

THE DEVELOPMENTAL PUEBLO

By 700 A.D., religious advances had led to a new trend in architecture. Stone and adobe construction replaced the traditional pithouses. The transition from pole and mud construction to contiguous flat-roofed adobe houses brought a new name. The Developmental (700–1050 A.D.) was the first of four "Pueblo" periods.

Initially the dwellings were single story. Later in the period, about 900 A.D., architects began designing storied homes with plazas adjoining in a common area. The pit remained a part of the structure, but it was now reserved for special events, with living quarters above ground. The underground rooms, called kivas, were entered by a ladder from the living area. At first the kivas were social areas with a fire pit in the center. As religion gained importance, the kivas become places of prayer and meditation in addition to their other uses.

Pottery reached new heights of craftsmanship during this period. Two general pot types characterize the period: the black and white design and the corrugated style. The corrugated style was made by coiling "ropes" of clay around and atop each other and pinching the coils together. This type of pot was especially good for cooking, as it drew and held heat from the fire.

The Neighbors

Puebloan ways of life were influencing cultures as far south as today's El Paso, Texas, and north and west from the Four Corners Area. Pithouse as well as pueblo dwelling remains have been found in southeastern Nevada. To the south, their influence extended into the Mogollon culture of New Mexico and Arizona. A distinct society at first, the Mogollon had, by the 700s, become blended with other cultures to such a degree that it lost its separate identity.

This "blended" culture was so amalgamated by 1000 A.D. that it is known by another name: Mimbres. The graves of the Mimbres have revealed some of the most distinctive pottery ever created. The black-on-white design and the artistic renderings of birds and animals have become the hallmark of Mimbres Pottery. Gravesites reveal pots with holes drilled or punched into them at the time of burial (the punched-out piece is also found in the grave). Apparently this procedure was to insure the release of the pot's soul, which was thought to be a part of its maker.

By the middle 1100s the Mimbres civilization had left the region. But another culture was coming under influence. From 500–700 A.D. in Arizona's San Francisco Mountains, and later than that in the Verde Valley, lived the Sinagua. Their name, meaning "without water," aptly describes the regions they inhabited. About 1066 A.D. an event occurred which would change the arid face of Sinagua territory.

While the Battle of Hastings was raging in England, Sunset Crater was erupting 15 miles northeast of Flagstaff, Arizona. The volcano covered the region with black ash, sending the Sinagua fleeing. But the ash proved to be a superb vehicle for trapping moisture, making the region's parched earth arable for raising crops. The revived farmland encouraged the Sinagua to return, and with them came Hohokam and Pueblo farmers, new settlers to this area.

By this time the Hohokam had reached the peak of their canal building near today's Phoenix. They were not as influenced by outside cultures as were certain other groups. But from the outsiders—possibly the Mayan Indians of Mexico—they learned a fascinating game. The rules are unclear, but teams competed to see who could knock a ball through rings mounted on earthen walls. The games may have been part of a religious ritual. At Snaketown on today's Gila Indian reservation, the remains of Hohokam ball courts can be seen.

Mesa Verde National Park　　　　　　　　SPRUCE TREE HOUSE

THE CLASSIC PUEBLO

The years 1050–1300 A.D. marked a golden age. During these 250 years the Pueblo People crafted their finest, most advanced pottery. They developed excellent methods of farming and irrigation, and generally lived a better life than at any other time in their history. Population at the three main centers increased as people from the outlying areas began moving in to form community groups.

To accommodate this change, the grand two-, three-, and four-story apartment-like buildings were constructed; for which they are best remembered. Clustered houses were arranged in a "stepped" fashion so the roof of one became the front porch for the one above. These dwellings had many rooms; Cliff Palace at Mesa Verde had more than 200, along with 23 kivas. Villages were built under the shallow overhangs of cliffs with several families comprising a community.

This time of good living was not to last. Whether they were starved out by drought and lack of crops, or driven out by conflict, or whether they simply left, no one is sure. Tree ring growth suggests a drought from 1276–1299. In this same period dwellings with a fort-like look were designed and there is evidence that Shoshonean tribe hunters were in the area, Whatever the reason, by 1300 the Pueblo dwellers were nearly gone from the Four Corners area.

SALADO AND CLASSIC HOHOKAM

The "Golden Age of Southern Arizona" occurred about the same time as the Classic Pueblo period in the north, beginning about 1200 A.D. Other cultures, particularly from the north had by now begun to influence Arizona's Hohokam people. About 1300 a new culture, the Salado, appeared in Hohokam lands. The Salado originated about 1100 A.D. in the Little Colorado area. Gradually they moved south toward the realm of the Hohokam.

The newcomers received a warm welcome. Despite the fact that there were three times as many Hohokam as Salado, the two cultures appear to have lived in peace for nearly 200 years. Each culture kept its distinctive qualities, but each also learned and benefitted from the other. The Salado, who seem to have had no experience in canal building, were good laborers for the Hohokam engineers and helped to bring construction to its height during this period.

Both cultures had pottery-making skills. Hohokam bowls were a plain tan or polished red color. Salado potters crafted some corrugated pots but most were a polychrome design with finishes of red, black, and white.

This period was one of slow growth in certain aspects of Hohokam culture. Apparently the ball games of earlier times were not as popular now, for the courts were smaller or non-existent. Certain crafts such as stone carving were not practiced as extensively.

In architecture the biggest changes of the 12th and 13th centuries occurred. The Hohokam began building thicker, more substantial walls in their dwellings. This allowed them to erect multi-storied buildings rather than the single-story units of earlier times. At Casa Grande National Monument in Arizona is a fine example of Hohokam construction.

One of the greatest differences in the two cultures was the way they disposed of their dead. The Salado preferred traditional burials, often using the plaza areas of their communities as cemeteries. The Hohokam cremated their dead, burning the bodies on a wooden grate over an open fire and placing the ashes in a clay pot for burial.

By 1400 the Salado had left the Gila River region, possibly heading east away from the newly arrived Apaches. It is not known what happened to the Hohokam. They may have become the ancestors of the modern-day Pima, for it was in Hohokam territory that Spanish explorers found the Pima in 1530.

Pecos National Historic Park   16th CENTURY POTTERY

THE PUEBLO IV PERIOD

And what of the civilization begun by the ancestral Puebloans? A portion of the people, by now called Pueblo Indians for the types of dwellings they built, migrated to the upper and middle Rio Grande regions and to the drainage of the Little Colorado. Here they built new communities, some even larger than those of the Classic Pueblo Period. Other Puebloans moved to existing pueblos at Acoma, Laguna, and Zuni in New Mexico and Hopi in Arizona. In general, the movement was south and east.

During the Pueblo IV period, the culture ceased to advance as it had in the previous 1300 years. While some of the dwellings built from 1300–1700 were substantial, an increasing number were not. Many were now made entirely of adobe and did not last long. Pottery and weaving were still high quality; a beautiful polychrome pottery was produced during these years. Kivas continued their importance as focal points of society. In fact, had it not been for the arrival of the Spanish in 1540, Puebloan culture might have seen a renaissance.

First came the explorer Coronado, searching for the Seven Cities of Gold. By 1598, Spanish settlers had entered the region. Their influence was tremendous—and disastrous to the Indians. So savagely were the Pueblos treated by the Spaniards that in 1680 a major uprising took place. The Indians drove the enemy out of their territory for 12 years. But in 1692 the Spanish returned, this time to overwhelm and occupy.

Mesa Southwest Museum   MODERN PUEBLO SANTA CLARA BLACKWARE

THE MODERN PUEBLO

No other southwestern Indians were successful in keeping the Spanish out of their lands for as long as the Pueblo. The Spanish were more organized and had better weapons than the Indians. But the Pueblo were defending their homeland.

As later white settlers would do, the Spanish took disgraceful advantage of the Pueblos. Missionaries tried to convert the "heathens." The Spanish attempted to introduce their own government into the native society. Settlers took the Pueblo into slavery and treated them savagely, stealing the natives' corn supply and trampling crops they didn't use. The resultant hunger coupled with disease against which the Indians had no defense, substantially reduced their population. During the 18th century, the number of Pueblo settlements dropped from 70 or 80 to 25 or 30.

Today's Pueblo are descendants of the Ancestral Puebloan tradition. After the Spanish invasion, they moved into eastern and western groups. The eastern lived in New Mexico pueblos like Taos along the Rio Grande and in the communities of Zuni, Acoma, and Laguna in the west central part of the state. The western division settled the Hopi villages of northern Arizona. The western Pueblo formed secret societies like the Kachina cults while easterners organized hunting societies. Although both adopted Spanish ways of farming and raising livestock, they retained their own culture to an amazing degree.

Mesa Verde National Park — COURTYARD, SPRUCE TREE HOUSE

MESA VERDE

We of the high-tech age may find it hard to comprehend how the ancestors of modern Pueblo Indians could build substantial architecture from sticks, stones, and sandstone. Yet using only the most primitive tools, the builders of Mesa Verde (*VURD* or *VAIR-day*) created such masterpieces as a 217-room living complex with 23 kivas. Today's travelers to southwestern Colorado's Mesa Verde National Park can view these remains at Cliff Palace, the largest cliff dwelling in North America.

Cliff Palace was constructed during the 13th century when dwellings were built under the edges of cliffs. Two cowboys, Richard Wetherill and Charlie Mason, first spotted it in 1888 as they rode the range on the Mesa top. Today one of the mesas in the park is named for Wetherill. The mesa of most intense occupation is named for Frederick H. Chapin, one of the first explorers into the area after its discovery.

It was not the Early Basketmakers but the Modified Basketmakers who were Mesa Verde's first residents. Along Mesa Top Drive, travelers can see the remains of pithouses from this period, the earliest permanent dwellings of Mesa Verdeans.

This same route allows travelers to experience 600 years of cultural development and architectural changes in a single drive. One site offers remnants from three periods—the poles of a pithouse stand near two pueblo structures dating to 1000 and 1075 A.D. Square Tower House, the tallest structure in the park, is also visible on this trip. This ruin was never a tower, but part of a multi-story dwelling occupied from 1200–1300.

Long House and Spruce Tree House are the second and third largest ruins of the several hundred at Mesa Verde. The latter was inhabited in the 13th century and, like Cliff Palace, was discovered by cowboys riding the mesa top. They gained entry by climbing down a large Douglas fir which sprouted from the ruin. A wall and raised courtyard separate the 114 rooms and eight kivas of Spruce Tree House from the main traffic area outside the cliff overhang. Travelers can inspect a kiva with a reconstructed roof by climbing down a wooden ladder.

For those who crave more climbing and crawling, Balcony House is a delightful visit. Tunnels, crevices, and long ladders invite travelers to explore this ruin, named for the balconies in the dwelling, which still exist. Actually these balconies were entryways into the second-story rooms.

At Balcony House is evidence of a problem that is prevalent in most cultures of the world: waste disposal. Trash was often simply thrown into the courtyards and walkways in front of the dwellings, and is particularly evident at Spruce Tree House. Sometimes the deep recesses of overhanging caves were used for trash, particularly human waste disposal. But amid these dumps were pottery shards and other treasures that have proven invaluable to archeologists.

To view these treasurers, travelers to Mesa Verde should stop at the Far View Visitor Center near the intersection of Wetherill Mesa and Chapin Mesa Roads. Here is information for planning a tour of major points in the Park. There is also a fine collection of modern southwest Indian crafts.

A drive south from the Visitor Center along the top of Chapin Mesa, takes the traveler to an area heavily populated from 900–1300. Water was a problem in this arid land, but the ancient residents seem to have had a solution. Atop the mesa sits Mummy Lake. During the height of habitation, it may have served as a reservoir.

Via a 3-mile round trip trail from the museum travelers can visit Petroglyph Point. Its original name, Pictograph Point, is incorrect for its illustrations are chipped into the rock (petroglyphs) rather than being painted onto it (pictographs). More than a dozen interconnected renderings illustrate religious symbols such as the sipapu. Their meanings have been interpreted for Park visitors by modern-day Hopi.

Greg Gnesios　　　　　　　　　　　　　　BALCONY HOUSE

On the Chapin Mesa loop which passes Spruce Tree House is the Archeological Museum. This makes an excellent orientation point for newcomers to the Park. Baskets, sandals, tools, and pottery show visitors what daily life was like at Mesa Verde nearly 700 years ago. The few baskets that have survived are from the Classic Pueblo period and not as high-quality as those of the earlier Basketmakers.

Pottery is where the women of Mesa Verde truly excelled. They made cups, ladles, pots, jars, water containers, and mugs. The corrugated or "pinched" pots were used for cooking and storage, whereas the beautifully designed black and white ware was reserved for special purposes. Examples of many different styles and designs are on exhibit at the Museum.

Tools made by the men are also on display. There are awls of bone, spear points and knives (some serrated) made of hard stream stones, bows and arrows from later periods, drills for tooling leather, scrapers for working hides, and more. Hides fashioned into robes with these tools, high-topped sandals lined with fur, and blankets made of turkey feathers offer visitors a picture of the winter attire of Mesa Verdeans.

Even foodstuffs have been found at Mesa Verde. Step House ruin on the Wetherill Mesa road is named for the entryway of rocks sloping down to the structure. Here archeologists recovered more than 1600 corn cobs as well as wild plant seeds—only part of a stash of food for four dozen or more people. Such remains give the traveler an intimate look at the lifestyle of the ancient of Mesa Verde.

Greg Gnesios   FREMONT PETROGLYPHS

DINOSAUR NATIONAL MONUMENT

Spanning the Utah-Colorado border to the north is another prehistoric site. At Dinosaur National Monument are remnants of the Fremont culture which occupied Utah from 100-1250 A.D. The Cub Creek site contains large numbers of petroglyphs and pictographs, remnants of the Fremont people.

Prior to the Fremont culture, an Archaic population lived here, from about 6000 B.C. to 200 A.D. These earlier people were skilled hunters, using an atlatl until 100 A.D. when the bow and arrow was introduced. Archaic sites are located at two areas of the monument known as Swelter Shelter and Deluge Shelter.

With the transition to Fremont culture came the introduction of ceramics. The early potters used a coil-and-scrape technique in their construction with limestone as temper. The pots were utilitarian and hence undecorated. Primitive pithouse remains also exist at Dinosaur. Archeologists have found indications of fire pits, storage areas, and postholes. Not until 400 A.D. was adobe introduced as a building material.

A variety of spear points and stone implements have been recovered from the sites. The Fremont people's reliance on hunting and gathering as well as on agriculture shows that the people planned a sedentary, year-round existence here in the canyons of the Green and Yampa Rivers.

Jim Court   SQUARE TOWER, HOVENWEEP NAT. MON.

HOVENWEEP NATIONAL MONUMENT

Straddling the Colorado-Utah border, directly west of Mesa Verde, lies Hovenweep National Monument. Ancestral Puebloans closely related to those that occupied Mesa Verde also lived in this region from approximately 500–1300 A.D. What distinguishes the ruins at Hovenweep from those of neighboring Mesa Verde are the tower-like structures. Just why these towers were built, archeologists cannot say. Some believe they were lookouts used to watch for enemies. Others think they were observatories for stargazing.

These intriguing towers were built of stone in four major designs: square, oval, round, and "D" shaped—a half-circle wall backed by a straight wall. Some ruins have only single towers with walls 20 feet high. Others display twin towers, often with rooms connecting them. All show a high level of architectural competence.

The Square Tower Ruins, just off Utah Highway 262, are the most accessible ruins at Hovenweep. Other ruins are isolated on gravel or dirt roads. Fortunately the Square Tower Ruins are the best preserved. This now arid land of silent ruins was abandoned, like other Ancestral Puebloan centers, about 1300. Today's Pueblo, Zuni, and Hopi Tribes are their descendants. The modern name Hovenweep is the Paiute/Ute Indian word for "deserted valley."

Greg Gnesios — BEEF BASIN, JUST OUTSIDE THE PARK

CANYONLANDS NATIONAL PARK

In the southeast corner of Utah, two of nature's master carvers—the Colorado and Green Rivers—have shaped sandstone into amazing geologic wonders that are the major attractions at Canyonlands. Human inhabitants have left their marks as well.

The Needles area in the southern part of the park has evidence of human habitation back 6000 years to the Archaic period, as well as evidence of Puebloan and Fremont people dating from 250 to 1350 A.D. At some rock art sites, such as Peek-a-Boo in the Needles District, white shield-bearing figures painted by late prehistoric people are superimposed on red Barrier Canyon rock art of the Archaic people. Several Archaic rock art panels are in the bottom of this canyon.

The Fremont probably followed the Archaic into the Canyonlands area. By early A.D. the Puebloans were in residence, the same culture group as at Mesa Verde and Chaco Canyon. They hunted and gathered, raised corn, squash, beans, and made tools and pottery. At Roadside Ruin in the Needles district are the remains of a granary. Other late prehistoric ruins can be seen at Aztec Butte in the Island in the Sky district and Tower Ruin in the Needles district. One of the best preserved remnants is Tower Ruin, located in the back country of Horse Canyon in the Needles section.

CAPITOL REEF NATIONAL PARK

Flowing east-west through Capitol Reef in south central Utah is the Fremont River. The prehistoric people who lived along it were given the river's name by an archeologist in the late 1920s. The Fremont people were almost exclusively Utah dwellers. Around the state there were five groups: the Great Salt Lake Fremont, the Parowan, the Uinta, the Sevier, and the San Rafael. The last group inhabited the Capitol Reef area from 700–1275 A.D., at the same time the Pueblo Culture was flourishing to the south.

Aspects of San Rafael Fremont life were similar to the Pueblo Culture, yet identifiable as a distinct culture. The Fremont built pithouses, remnants of which can be seen today at Capitol Reef. Although they were not cave dwellers, they did use caves for storage. They made pottery, primarily plain black or gray, and later in the period produced some black on white. They also made unfired clay figures, many in human shapes, for use in ceremonial rites. Another interesting Fremont creation was a type of moccasin constructed from three pieces of hide. These moccasins incorporated the animal's dewclaws—those useless inner claws—for just what reason, archeologists aren't sure!

But the most distinctive feature of the Fremont culture—and the most prevalent reminder today of their existence in the West—is their rock art. Thousands of examples exist at Capitol Reef. Human beings shaped like trapezoids are a frequent theme. Often the artist decorated his humans with jewelry or shields. Bighorn sheep and other game animals are common in hunting scenes.

The Capitol Reef area in which much of this rock art is found is a true geologic wonder. Located here is a giant wrinkle in the Earth's crust called Waterpocket Fold. The same geologic uplift which created the Colorado Plateau also forced layers of once-horizontal rock and sediment in Capitol Reef to bend. Erosion ultimately wore away the top layers, but in the process spectacular cliffs, spires, domes and canyons were created. It is on the walls of these that much of the Fremont rock art can be found.

The questions that surround the end of the Ancestral Pueblo culture also engulf the Fremont people. Some say they left the Capitol Reef region to join other cultures such as the Plains Indians to the east or the emerging Paiutes. Other archeologists, believe the Fremonts were simply a segment of Pueblo Culture, and say they went south about 1275 to join the Pueblo migrations.

Utah Museum of Natural History — FREMONT FIGURINES

SITES ADMINISTERED BY THE STATE OF UTAH

The Utah Department of Parks Recreation and Tourism oversees a number of prehistoric Indian sites of interest to the traveler. In southeastern Utah is **Newspaper Rock**, a state historic park named for the large petroglyph panel preserved there. Making up the rock art are hundreds of figures and characters.

South of Newspaper Rock near Blanding is **Edge of the Cedars**, a state park and museum. The focal point of this site is a pueblo containing 75 surface rooms and 10 kivas. From 750–1220 A.D., a small village was located here. The museum contains an extensive collection of Puebloan pottery as well as exhibits on contemporary Indians such as the Navajo and Ute.

In central Utah near Boulder is **Anasazi State Park** site of a prehistoric Puebloan village. Pottery shards indicate occupation here from 1050 to 1200 A.D. This culture apparently associated with the Kayenta then living in northeastern Arizona. During excavation, 87 rooms were uncovered. In addition there is a full-sized replica of a dwelling along with a museum of artifacts from this site.

Excellent rock art of the Fremont Indians is also preserved at **Fremont Indian State Park** off I-70 near Sevier. Here lies the largest Fremont village yet unearthed, including 80 homesites, several granaries and tons of pottery, arrowheads and artifacts.

Bureau of Land Management PAROWAN GAP PETROGLYPHS

OFF THE BEATEN PATH SITES IN UTAH

Parowan Gap Petroglyphs: This large, well-preserved group of petroglyphs (pecked, not painted!) is managed by the Cedar City Field Office of Bureau of Land Management. The artists were from the early Fremont culture or possibly earlier Archaic hunters and gatherers. Parowan Fremont established long-term villages here and subsisted on farming from approximately 700–1200. Many petroglyphs are accessible.

South Fork Indian Canyon Pictographs: A large rock shelter with painted rock art panels. Site is open to the public but difficult to access. Contains figures of humans and animals painted in red, yellow, and white pigments. Some remains date to 280 A.D. The site is managed by BLM's Kanab Field Office

Red Cliffs: The cliffs provided the early inhabitants protection from harsh winter winds. The Red Cliffs site was inhabited from about 600-1050, has been professionally excavated and is open to the public. This Archeological Site is managed by the St. George Field Office of Bureau of Land Management

Butler Wash: Abandoned about 1300, the site is interesting for its kivas. There are four; three round kivas similar to those found at Mesa Verde and a fourth square kiva more typical of the Kayenta culture to the south. BLM's Monticello Field Office manages the Butler Wash, Mule Canyon, Sand Island and Three Kiva Pueblo Sites.

Mule Canyon: A canyon filled with prehistoric sites including an excavated village with a two-story tower, two kivas and twelve rooms. All the ruins have been stabilized and permanent displays made.

Sand Island: The rock art panel at Sand Island is extensive and represents images from 800 to 2500 years old. It presents an overview of the type of rock art that is found all along the San Juan River. A boat trip on the river leads to well-preserved cliff dwellings with views of Rock art, pottery fragments and stone tools.

Three Kiva Pueblo: Located in Montezuma Canyon, this site was occupied 1000-1300. Three kivas and 14 rooms have been excavated and stabilized.

(for location of these sites see the map on page 24-25)

National Park Service ARCHES NATIONAL PARK

OTHER UTAH SITES

Because prehistoric Indians were often nomadic, archeologists have found evidence of their cultures where there were never any permanent settlements. **Arches National Park** in southeast Utah is one such site. What is now the park was once the northern extremity of ancestral Puebloan territory. Hunters following game visited here but did not stay. Archeologists have also found evidence of visits from Fremont, Ute, Paiute and Shoshoneans. Just outside the park on Highway 191 is the **Moab Rock Art Panel**, a series of pictographs painted in the traditional Fremont style.

Sharing the Utah/Wyoming border in the northeast corner of Utah is **Flaming Gorge National Recreation Area**. Here, too, is evidence of prehistoric visitation. Archeologists have found petroglyphs and other artifacts indicating that early man hunted in this region for many centuries.

Surrounding Flaming Gorge is the **Ashley National Forest**. The Fremont culture was active here and some evidence of their habitation has been found. Ute Indians lived here in the 19th and early 20th centuries.

Natural Bridges National Monument, 40 miles west of Blanding, Natural Bridges National Monument protects three major natural bridges, geologic features carved by running water. Living here in prehistoric times were peoples culturally like their ancestral Puebloan neighbors to the east. White Canyon was a major center and at Horsecollar Ruin are the remains of their structures. Armstrong Canyon also had ancestral inhabitants. In the 1200s, farmers from Mesa Verde migrated here, but by the 1300s they migrated south. During later times, Navajos and Paiutes lived in the area. but both the canyons are too narrow to allow much farming.

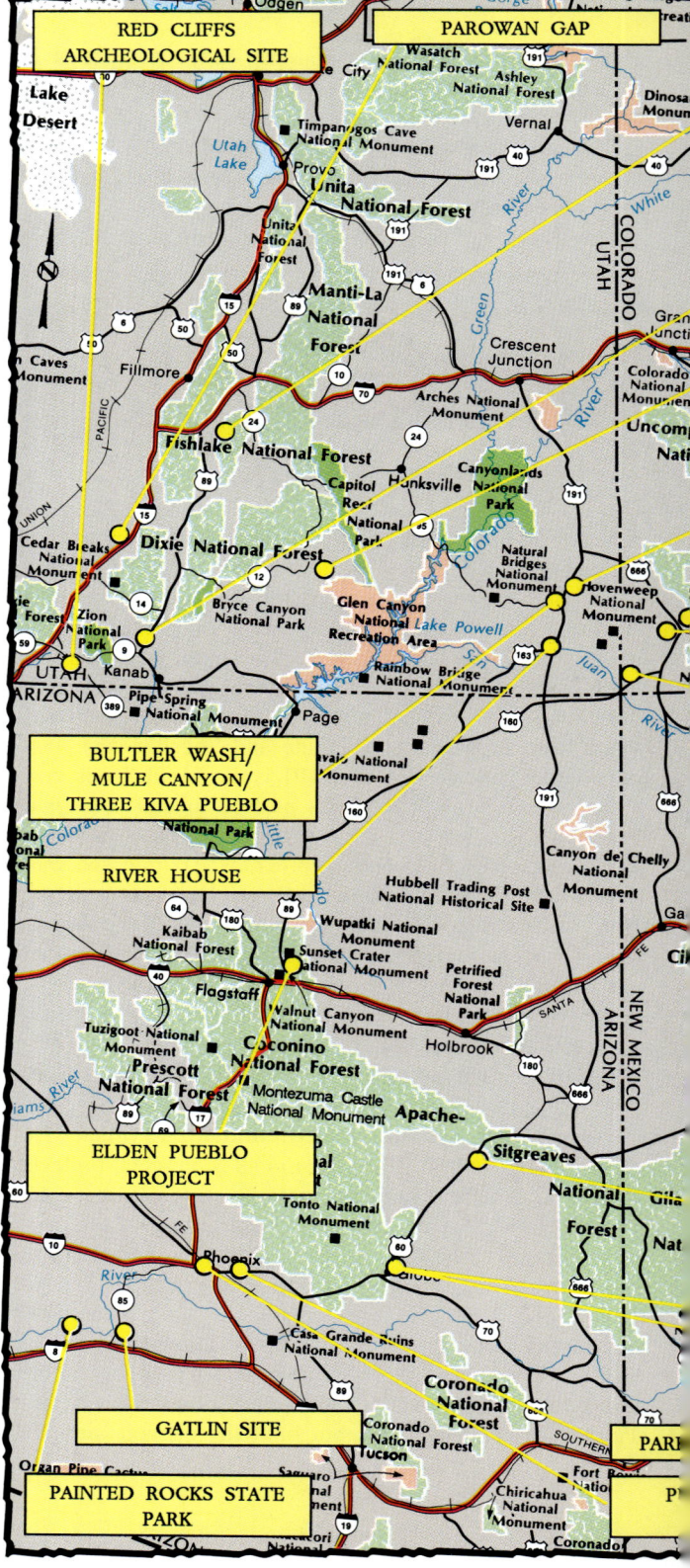

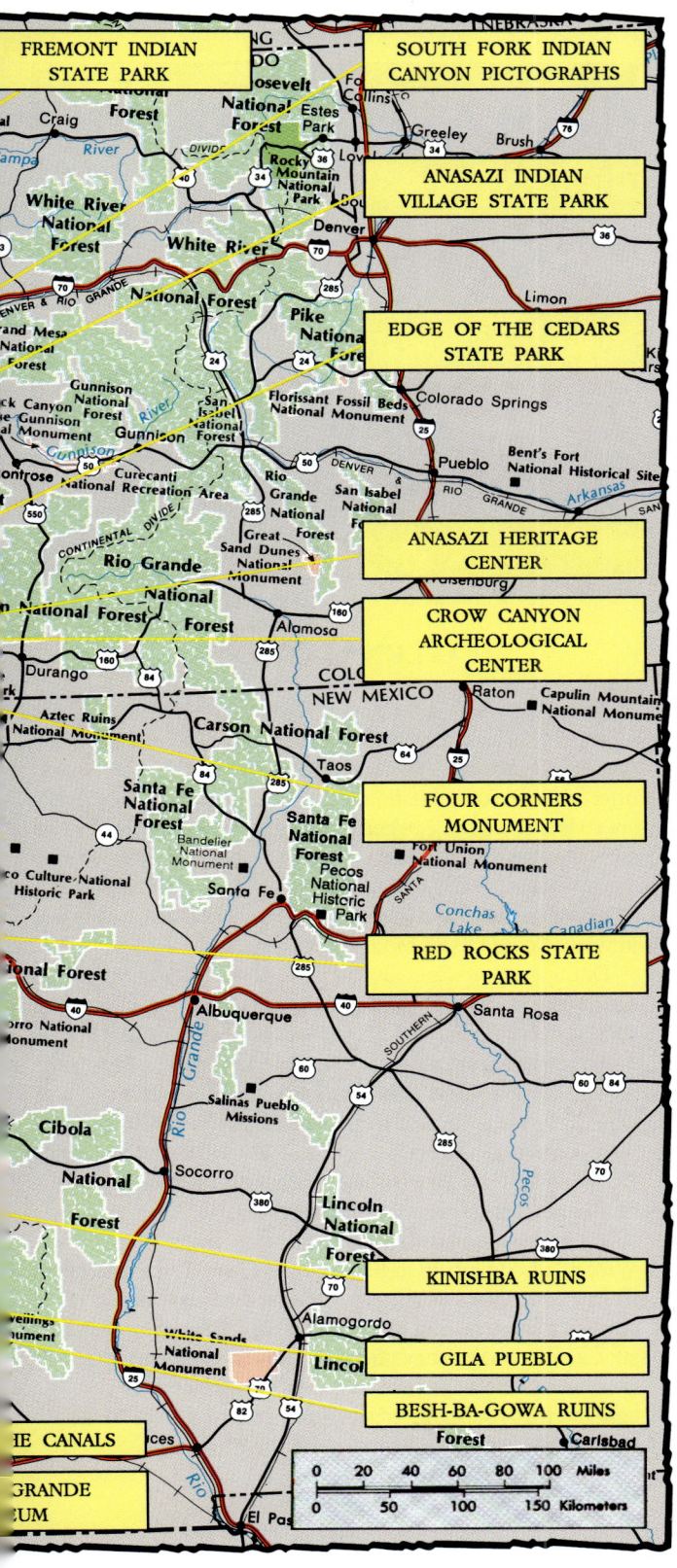

Glen Canyon N.R.A.   DEFIANCE HOUSE RUIN

GLEN CANYON

What is today Glen Canyon National Recreation Area in the Four Corners region of Arizona and Utah was once an Ancestral homeland. Two major sites and a variety of remains offer evidence of habitation. One of the best preserved, Defiance House, was an isolated, untouched ruin until 1959 when archeologists discovered it in Forgotten Canyon. Perched atop a steep slope 200 feet above the canyon floor were the remains of a kiva, granary, and living area. In a corner were two bowls in which some bits of food still remained.

Defiance House gets its name from the pictographs on a nearby cliff. Three defiant warriors holding clubs and shields decorate the rock. Just why the people settled here is a mystery to archeologists. The site is protected from the elements and remote enough to deter enemies. But it is also a quarter mile from any water source. Perhaps this is why it was populated for only 35 years. By 1285 the Defiance House dwellers, like other Ancestral Puebloans in the region had abandoned their homes.

Another major site—the largest at Glen Canyon—is Widow's Ledge Ruin in Slickrock Canyon. It was occupied from 1210 until the large-scale abandonment about 1300. Among the interesting items found here were gaming pieces such as dice, paint sticks used by the early pictograph painters, cotton cloth and anchor points for looms. The site contained 20 rooms, granaries, and perhaps a kiva. Ruins are open to the public, but access is quite difficult.

Bob Bradshaw   BETATAKIN RUIN

NAVAJO NATIONAL MONUMENT

Of the three main groups of Ancestral Puebloans—the Mesa Verde, the Chaco, and the Kayenta—the third group chose parts of Arizona and southeastern Utah as its home. A major Kayenta settlement was in Tsegi Canyon, now Navajo National Monument, on the Navajo Indian reservation in northern Arizona.

The Kayentans arrived here about 300 A.D., the first groups making their homes near flowing water in the canyon bottoms. Three of the best preserved cliff dwellings in the southwest are here. Betatakin (meaning "ledge house") contained 135 rooms and was inhabited for about 50 years beginning in 1250. Some of the paintings on the surrounding cliffs may have been done by the early Kayentans or by later Indian dwellers.

Ruins visible today were built after 1250 when a community was established at Keet Seel (meaning "broken pieces of pottery.") This collection of pueblo dwellings ultimately had 160 rooms. Keet Seel and Betatakin were among the last of the great cliff dwellings to be occupied in the San Juan drainage. In 1286, the last trees were cut for roofing and by 1300, most of the cliff dwellings had been abandoned. A third major ruin in the monument, Inscription House, dates to the same period but is closed because of its fragility and difficult public access.

Kevin McKibbin   KEET SEEL RUIN

Kayenta pueblo construction was not as advanced as that of other Puebloans. Builders used irregularly shaped stones, which meant their dwellings required large quantities of mortar to stay together. A distinctive characteristic of Kayenta settlements was the kivas. Ruins at Keet Seel exemplify the circular kiva style, but without the pillars or shafts of stone common to Mesa Verde kiva construction. At Keet Seel the six ceremonial structures illustrate the diversity in construction, from keyhole, to rectangular, round, and even tear-drop shaped.

The Kayenta made beautiful black-on-white pottery, but some of their corrugated ware was inferior to that of the Mesa Verde or Chaco groups. The Kayenta used intricate patterns and incorporated so many black designs that the pieces sometimes appeared to be white-on-black. The Kayenta are also known for polychrome wear which utilized a yellow or red base with red, black, or white designs. A wide red stripe with black or white borders was particularly characteristic of this group.

There are many theories as to why the Four Corners region was abandoned. Drought and possible enemy infiltration are most often mentioned. But scientists now believe that erosion due to soil overuse to feed growing populations, along with social collapse, may have largely caused the exodus. Inhabitants abandoned Keet Seel beginning in the late 1200s and were gone by 1300. Apparently they planned to return, for some sealed their doors, leaving pottery jars with seed corn in the rooms.

Canyon de Chelly N.M.   CANYON de CHELLY

CANYON DE CHELLY

Also located on the Navajo reservation is Canyon de Chelly (*SHAY*) National Monument. Scattered throughout the monument are thousands of pictographs and petroglyphs, the record of Puebloan Ancestors who lived here for more than 1000 years. Pictographs are in greater abundance for they were easier to execute than the carving/scratching technique of petroglyphs.

For their pigments, the artists used natural colored clays, with charcoal for gray and black highlights. Thickening agents for the paints included natural oils, egg whites, blood, even urine. Yucca fiber or animal hair made good brushes. The many overhanging rocks at Canyon de Chelly have protected the artists' work, some of which dates to 350 A.D.

Remains of ancestral structures also exist at the monument. In Canyon del Muerto (Canyon of the Dead) are Antelope House and Mummy Cave. Ruins at the latter site, confirmed by tree ring dating, were built in 348 A.D. and are the earliest structures in the San Juan drainage area. Also found here are some of the last buildings to be built by the Puebloan Ancestors, dating to 1284. Of equal interest to the traveler is the awesome White House Ruin. Modern Navajo Indians who today inhabit Canyon de Chelly act as tour guides to the many ancient ruins.

Mesa Southwest Museum   MANO, GRINDING STONE W/LIZARD FIGURE

GRAND CANYON NATIONAL PARK

The beauty and size of the Grand Canyon has welcomed human inhabitants to this region for 4000 years, maybe longer. Tiny figurines made of split willow twigs offer clues to the Pinto Basin-Desert people, some of the earliest dwellers. This segment of the Desert Culture hunted with spears and slept under rock overhangs, traveling up and down the canyon walls as a matter of course in everyday life.

Little is known of the period following the Pinto people. But about 500 A.D., the Basketmakers lived here and evolved into an agricultural society. Farming supplied about half the food needs of the people. To supplement their diet, hunters using bows and arrows killed deer and big horn sheep while women and children gathered nuts and berries. During the Pueblo period, canyon dwellers built irrigation devices to increase their yield from farming.

More than 2000 habitation sites have been found in the Grand Canyon. On the South Rim the Tusayan Pueblo (part of the Kayenta culture) has been excavated. This community was developed about 1185. The main structure had 15 rooms, seven for living quarters and the rest for storage.

About 1300, these ancestors of the modern-day Hopi migrated east. Today, seven miles below the rim in a side canyon, Havasupai Indians live. The reservation's single village, Supai, is the last place in the United States where mail is delivered by mule.

Russ Finley   WUKOKI RUIN

WUPATKI & SUNSET CRATER

Oxidized iron and sulfur scoria spilling over the volcano lip have left the red and yellow pattern which gives Sunset Crater, north of Flagstaff, Arizona its name. Explorer John Wesley Powell was the first European to observe this sunset effect when he visited the crater some 800 years after its 1064–65 eruption. Prior to the eruption, Sinagua people lived here. But when Mother Nature wreaked havoc upon them, they left.

Intermittently for 200 years the volcano continued its spewing. During this time the Sinagua returned, along with the Kayenta people. The combined cultures produced advancements in agriculture, pottery, and home building techniques. Volcanic ash in the soil and climatic changes after the eruption may have improved farmers' yields. For nearly 125 years these cultures prospered. But about 1225 they left, probably traveling north to the Hopi mesas and south as well.

Today's travelers can visit "Wupatki" (Hopi for "tall house"). This ruin is one of more than 2,668 sites in the monument. It is multi-storied and contains more than 100 rooms. Perched on a big boulder is another large (possibly three-family) ruin, "Wukoki," meaning "big house." More than 50 different types of pottery from various prehistoric people have been found here. Archeologists think this variety is the result of heavy trading among prehistoric peoples of the Southwest.

Greg Gnesios   MONTEZUMA WELL

MONTEZUMA CASTLE & TUZIGOOT

The Verde Valley area south of Flagstaff once bustled with prehistoric activity and is the site of Montezuma Castle National Monument. About 600 A.D. the Hohokam settled here and developed sophisticated irrigation methods for farming. They lived in single-room pole-and-mud houses. A short distance away, in the Flagstaff area, were the Sinagua, dryland farmers who depended on rainfall. When the Hohokam left their green valley about 1125 to test the new volcanic soil of the Wupatki area, the Sinagua moved in, adopting the irrigation methods of the former inhabitants.

From their northern neighbors, the Sinagua learned masonry construction to replace their pithouses. By 1150 they were building large pueblos. The most spectacular ruin from this period is a 5-story, 20-room dwelling perched 100 feet up the side of a cliff. Visitors to Montezuma Castle National Monument can view this and other remains of the culture that reached its peak here about 1300.

A short distance north is Montezuma Well, a limestone sink created by the collapse of a subterranean cavern. Underground springs that fill the well also supplied water to the Hohokam and Sinagua. Ruins of dwellings built between 1100 and 1400 can be seen there. Northwest at Tuzigoot National Monument (Apache meaning "crooked water") the remains of a Sinagua village from the same period sit on a ridge high above the valley. Settlers fleeing the drought of the 1200s and 1300s settled at Tuzigoot, greatly expanding its population.

Russ Finley — INTERIOR OF RUINS

TONTO NATIONAL MONUMENT

Taking their name from the Rio Salado (Salt River) which flowed through their homeland east of Phoenix were the Salado people, a culture whose remains are today preserved at Tonto National Monument. There was nomadic human activity here as early as 5000 B.C., but by 850 A.D. the Hohokam had made this area their home. Here they lived in pithouses until about 1150. By that time their housing, pottery, and other ways of life had changed so much that they could no longer be called Hohokam. The new culture which emerged was the Salado.

Thanks to their knowledge of irrigation, the Salado were able to raise beans, cotton, corn, and other products. Below the siltstone cliffs they built pueblo villages, constructing multi-story dwellings of rocks and mud. Today's travelers can view the Lower Ruin, a structure of 16 lower rooms, three of them having an upper story. A 12-room annex stands nearby. The Upper Ruin, also located at Tonto, has 32 rooms on the first floor and eight on the second. The roofs of the lower level rooms made terraces for the upper levels.

These ruins, along with pottery shards and bits of fabric, have helped archeologists piece together the Salado culture. These early people stayed in the area about 300 years, until the first half of the 15th century. Why they left remains a mystery.

National Park Service   CASA GRANDE RUINS

CASA GRANDE

One of the largest structures of prehistoric America still stands north of Coolidge, Arizona. Casa Grande is a four-story building made of caliche, a lime based soil found in desert climates. Built by the Hohokam about 1350, it is nevertheless a Mexican-style structure, not consistent with Hohokam architecture. The builders did not use bricks, but simply piled up a wall of the caliche mixture, let it dry, and added onto it.

The purpose of Casa Grande is unclear. It was probably not a dwelling, but more likely designed for a special function. Openings in the walls of the upper floors suggest that it might have been an astronomical observatory. Whatever its purpose, the structure was used only for a century.

By 1450, Casa Grande and the other 60 sites surrounding it were abandoned by the Hohokam. It is not clear what caused the abandonment of large Hohokam villages. Water was an ever-present concern in this country, but the Hohokam were adept at constructing irrigation systems. They and their ancestors built more than 600 miles of canals, most three feet deep and of varying widths.

Today six of the many prehistoric villages at the monument have been excavated. Modern **Tohono O'odam** Indians of Arizona are descendants of the Hohokam which means "those who have gone" in their language.

Charles Busby   PUERCO RUINS, PETRIFIED FOREST N.P.

OTHER ARIZONA SITES

Petrified Forest National Park is best-known for its logs, long-ago infiltrated with silica deposits which hardened them into stone-like pieces of petrified wood. But the area also contains relics of human habitation. **Newspaper Rock** preserves many petroglyphs believed to be solar observations of the Puebloan Ancestors who lived here from 700–1450. At **Puerco Pueblo** is a stone "calendar" where sunlight shines through cracks in the rocks onto petroglyphs to mark the progression of the year.

In Phoenix is **Pueblo Grande Museum and Archaeological Park,** located on the site of a Hohokam ruin complete with irrigation canals and a prehistoric ball court. Nearby in Mesa is **Park of the Canals** which also preserves a Hohokam irrigation system. The later Mormon settlers re-used these prehistoric canals.

Near Gila Bend at **Painted Rocks State Park** are outstanding Indian petroglyphs. **Gatlin Site** is a Hohokam village preserving pithouses, ball courts, middens (trash heaps), and prehistoric canals. On the Fort Apache Indian reservation are the **Kinishba Ruins**, a Mogollon settlement with over 400 rooms. Southwest near Globe is the **Gila Pueblo**, a 14th century Salado structure of more than 200 rooms. Also at Globe is **Besh-Ba-Gowah Archaeological Park** containing Salado ruins from 1225 to 1400 A.D.

National Park Service — GILA CLIFF DWELLINGS

GILA CLIFF DWELLINGS

This national monument in southwestern New Mexico preserves ruins from the Mogollon people who lived here for nearly 1300 years. The oldest ruin is a pithouse dating to the period 100–400 A.D., the floor of which is below ground level. But many other masonry or adobe pithouses at the monument, built later in the period, are above-ground structures.

About 1270 A.D. the Mogollon began building their homes in natural caves. In a canyon along the West Fork of the Gila River are seven such caves, accessible via a one-mile walking trail. Five of them contain ruins of stone cliff dwellings consisting of about 40 rooms. These structures were home to 10 or 15 families at a time and they were used by several generations of Mogollon.

The Mogollon crafted two major styles of pottery. The earlier people made plain brown pots. After 1000 A.D. they developed a white pottery with black designs. They also made distinctive brown bowls with black interiors.

Mogollon women were expert weavers. In addition to sandals, they wove cotton into blankets and breechclouts. The men farmed, raising the staple crops as well as amaranth and tobacco. But by the early 1300s the Mogollon had abandoned their homes for reasons unknown.

Russ Finley ATSINNA AT EL MORRO

EL MORRO NATIONAL MONUMENT

In northwestern New Mexico, a huge sandstone bluff has marked the way for travelers for many centuries. El Morro ("the bluff") was the relocation point for many displaced Puebloans who moved from the Colorado Plateau region in the late 1200s.

They came to El Morro in search of a reliable water supply and better soil for farming. Volcanic ash in the area provided good soil. The nearby Zuni River, plus the mesa top advantage of better precipitation, combined to insure sufficient water. At the base of El Morro is a large watering hole, known to all since the early inhabitants.

By 1275 a population of 1,500 had established a village on the bluff top that modern historians named Atsinna, "writings on the rock." Here at Inscription Rock and on other nearby cliff walls, archeologists found petroglyphs of birds, animals, and other designs. Later Spanish and Anglo travelers added their artwork and messages to the rock.

The ruin at Atsinna is huge. Built on three levels, it had 500 rooms at the first level, 250 at the second, and 125 at the third. Archeologists think that about 65% of the rooms were inhabited at any one time, the rest being used for storage. By 1350 the Puebloans had begun to leave the area, heading for what is today the Zuni Pueblo of New Mexico.

National Park Service — PECOS NATIONAL HISTORIC PARK

PECOS NATIONAL HISTORIC PARK

Where did the Puebloans go in the 13th and 14th centuries? Archeologists are not sure. Evidence indicates that many migrated south and east in search of better soil or more reliable water supplies. About 1100 A.D. a group of Pueblo left the Rio Grande Valley and settled in the Pecos River Valley of New Mexico.

During the 1300s the people moved into pueblos of one and two stories. They raised beans, squash, and corn, irrigating with water from the Pecos River. What made their village quite prosperous was its location. On one side were the buffalo-hunting Indians of the plains. On the other were the sedentary farmers of the Rio Grande. The Pueblo of the Pecos Valley traded with both groups acquiring, among other goods, cotton that they could not raise themselves.

The Pueblo were also good warriors. On this site they built a four-and five-story pueblo that provided very good defense. The economy prospered. In 1540, when Coronado and his Spanish explorers arrived, en route to the famed Seven Cities of Cibola, they found a village of nearly 2000 Indians. This was the beginning of conflict and compromise between the native peoples and the Spanish. The remains of a 17th and 18th century mission erected by Spanish priests are today the most spectacular sights at the Pecos National Historic Park in Pecos, New Mexico.

Petly Studios   SAN BUENAVENTURA MISSION

SALINAS PUEBLO MISSIONS

Two ancient cultures of the southwest, the Puebloans and the Mogollon, once inhabited the Salinas Valley of New Mexico. Their ancestors dated back 7000 years. Before them, as long ago as 20,000 years, were the nomadic cultures. The Mogollon had established villages here by the 10th century, subsisting on simple farming as well as hunting and gathering. It is they who developed the red/brown pottery.

During the late 12th century, the Puebloans from the Colorado Plateau began to influence the already established Mogollon in the area. Stone and adobe structures began to dominate the prehistoric villages as they emerged into Pueblo societies. By 1300 the Salinas Valley dwellers had adopted adobe *jacales*, above-ground dwellings like pithouses built of poles covered with adobe. Later they constructed larger dwellings of stone arranged around a plaza or central courtyard and interspersed with kivas. The Pueblo culture also influenced weaving, basketry, and black-on-white pottery making in the Salinas Valley.

Ultimately the Salinas Valley became an important center for trade. In the 17th century archeologists estimate that 10,000 people lived here. Still, the area never reached the level of cultural development that the Puebloans to the north achieved. By the 1670s intrusions by the Spanish, Zuni, Apaches, and other outside influences became overwhelming and the Salinas villages were deserted.

Chris Judson, National Park Service   TALUS HOUSE, BANDELIER N.M.

BANDELIER NATIONAL MONUMENT

Named for Adolph Bandelier, the Swiss-born self-taught archeologist who first explored here, these ruins mark some of the last periods of prehistoric Indian culture in the Southwest. When Bandelier arrived, the Pueblo Indians were living in the Santa Fe area. He studied their culture and that of their ancestors. Most of Bandelier's findings date to the late pre-Spanish period, with some going back to the 12th century. Much of his work was done on the Pajarito (Little Bird) Plateau and in Frijoles (Bean) Canyon.

The canyon is today one of the most accessible parts of the monument, 90 percent of which is wilderness. In the main ruins area are the excavated sites of Tyuonyi and Long House, villages occupied until the mid-1500s by descendants of the Ancestrial Puebloans who migrated from the Four Corners area. When drought, a decline in trade with neighbors to the south, and an increasing density of population forced them to move from their home areas, many relocated to this region of the northern Rio Grande drainage between the Jemez and the Sangre de Cristo ranges.

For nearly 400 years, the Indians farmed the mesa tops and built cliff dwellings in the canyon walls. When the Conquistador Coronado arrived in 1540, the villages were abandoned, their people having moved to other areas. Today their descendants live in various Rio Grande pueblos.

Russ Finley, Chaco Culture N.H.P. ROOMS AND KIVA

CHACO CULTURE NATIONAL HISTORIC PARK

One of the three great centers of ancestral Puebloan culture was the remote and isolated Chaco Canyon in northwestern New Mexico. Today the site is a national historic park located 73 miles south of Aztec. Here, beginning about 900 A.D., the culture refined and focused its social, political and economic energies. The Chaco group's social development and architecture reached levels rarely attained by other peoples of the Four Corners region.

It appears that Chaco was a sort of capital for this area, acting perhaps as a storage and distribution center for agricultural products. Population estimates vary, for the canyon may have been used seasonally by people from throughout the region, but somewhere between 2000 and 5000 people once lived in this area. A smaller resident population may have occupied the sites along the 10-mile stretch of canyon. They settled in some 400 prehistoric villages of varying sizes. Chaco was about midway north-south, in the eastern sector.

Just why a people so dependent on agriculture would settle in this desert climate with long winters, archeologists are not certain, but they adapted to their dry climate with an ingenious irrigation system. To protect themselves against an often short growing season, they stored the harvests from good years in anticipation of times of need.

Russ Finley, Chaco Culture N.H.P.   EAST WING, PUEBLO BONITO

Another architectural and engineering accomplishment was a complex of prehistoric roads associated with the great house structures. These roads were not merely foot paths. They were planned and engineered highways averaging 30 feet in width and encompassing 400 miles. Most construction was done during the 11th and 12th centuries. The roads helped to tie people of the various settlements around Chaco into one cohesive culture.

A possible stimulus for the sophisticated road system may have been the extensive trading network in which Chacoans engaged. People traded among themselves, with people of other villages and with cultures as far away as Mexico. Much of the black and white Cibola pottery associated with the Chaco culture was likely imported. In trade, Chacoans were likely to offer some of their finely crafted turquoise jewelry, more of which has been discovered here than at any other site in the Southwest. Chacoans, like other prehistoric groups, incorporated sea shells into their jewelry designs, leading archeologists to assume that they had traded with people from coastal areas.

A hallmark of the Chaco culture was architecture, which dramatically increased in scale and mass in the early 900s. The first buildings at the Chaco sites had walls which were one stone thick, held together by much mortar. Travelers can see this earliest type of construction at Pueblo Bonito, the largest of the Chaco Canyon ruins. Ultimately this pueblo would consist of 600 rooms and 40 kivas, extending four stories high.

In building these multi-story dwellings, Chacoans knew they needed a more substantial wall than the one-stone-thick variety. Thus they began building walls around a core

Russ Finley, Chaco Culture N.H.P.   WALL CONSTRUCTION

made of rubble and mortar fragments. On the outside of this core, builders used a structural or load-bearing veneer of stone. The walls were tapered as they rose, another indication of the sophistication of Chaco architects.

Kin Kletso ruin, built in the early 12th century, exemplifies a type of construction called McElmo, a change from previous styles. A softer, lighter sandstone, which required extensive shaping and surface finishing, was selected as a building material. The first buildings here were built about 1125; the later ones about five years later. In all, this multi-story pueblo consisted of 100 rooms with five kivas.

Chaco Canyon is filled with other huge ruins. Una Vida near the visitor center was begun near the start of the Chaco settlement period and has about 150 rooms with five kivas. Chetro Ketl contains approximately 500 rooms, 16 kivas, and an enclosed plaza. Pueblo del Arroyo has roughly 280 rooms and more than 20 kivas. The focal point of park kivas is Casa Rinconada, largest of the great kivas.

The use of Chaco as a center of culture declined just as other areas such as Mesa Verde and the little Colorado drainage were booming. The center's population dwindled as people moved elsewhere in search of more dependable agricultural conditions, for not only had there been a drought, after many generations of land overuse, residents were seeing a strain on the Plateau's environment.

Aztec Ruins N.M. CORNER DOORWAYS ON UPPER AZTEC STORIES

AZTEC RUINS NATIONAL MONUMENT

Located in far northwestern New Mexico, this national monument marks what was once the center point between two great ancestral Puebloan centers. Just to the north in Colorado was Mesa Verde. Sixty-five miles south was the Chaco Canyon center. The Chaco culture peaked between 1050 and 1150. The Aztec community was one of many Chaco "outliers," part of the highly organized Chaco system. It was used as a trade and ceremonial center.

These people were farmers, relying on the nearby Animas River for rich land and water. At the area's height during the Chaco period, several hundred people lived here. But between 1175 and 1200, for reasons possibly related to the drought of the late 1100s, the Chaco left. Until 1225 the pueblo was uninhabited. Mesa Verde settlers then arrived with a slightly different culture. Pieces of pottery exemplify differences in the two cultures. Mesa Verdeans also introduced T-shaped doors and unique kiva styles. But within 50 years they, too, had abandoned Aztec.

Today the West Ruin, a huge multi-story pueblo with approximately 500 rooms, reminds travelers of the ambitious construction done here by the first settlers in the early 1100s. Perhaps the most impressive structure was the Great Kiva with its 41-foot diameter, built by the Chaco and remodeled by later residents.

PLANNING YOUR TRAVEL
FOUR CORNERS
Here you can be in four different states at the same time. Arizona, Colorado, New Mexico and Utah, the states that share the Ancestral Puebloan Culture.

UTAH
ANASAZI INDIAN STATE PARK, Boulder
This village site was occupied from about 1050 to 1200. Largely unexcavated, many artifacts have been uncovered and are on display in the park's museum.

ARCHES NATIONAL PARK, Moab
Hunter-gatherers migrated into the area about 10,000 years ago at the end of the Ice Age. As they explored , they found pockets of rock perfect for making stone tools.

ASHLEY NATIONAL FOREST, Vernal
Ancient Paleoindians hunted along the Green River 10,000 years ago. Later, Fremont farmers stored their corn in hidden granaries on canyon walls.

BRYCE CANYON NATIONAL PARK
Pueblo peoples hunted game in Bryce Canyon's forests and meadows. Paiutes frequented the plateau to harvest pine nuts and hunt rabbits.

CANYONLANDS NATIONAL PARK, Moab
The Ancestral Puebloans who once occupied Tower Ruin selected a neighborhood offering both beauty and practicality.

CAPITOL REEF NATIONAL PARK, Torrey
Elaborately decorated Fremont clay figurines, pictographs and petroglyphs have been found in abundance here. The figures include people, animals and abstract designs.

COLLEGE OF EASTERN UTAH PREHISTORIC MUSEUM, Price
Museum features the archeology and paleontology of eastern Utah's ancestral cultures. A major attraction is the Pilling Figurines from the Fremont culture.

EDGE OF THE CEDARS STATE PARK, Blanding
Occupied from 700 to 1200, Edge of the Cedar Indian Ruin was an agricultural village. The park museum features an excellent interpreted pottery collection.

FLAMING GORGE NATIONAL RECREATION AREA, Manila
Petroglyphs and artifacts found here suggest that Fremont Indians hunted game near the gorge for many centuries. Later, the Comanche, Shoshoni, and Ute tribes visited.

FREMONT INDIAN STATE PARK, Sevier
The Park preserves Clear Creek Canyon's treasury of Fremont pictographs and petroglyphs and archaeological relics. A visitor center and museum are on site.

HOVENWEEP NATIONAL MONUMENT, Blanding
Protects six prehistoric, Puebloan-era villages spread over a twenty-mile expanse of mesa tops and canyons.

HUCK'S MUSEUM, Blanding
Displays Indian artifacts from the last 1000 years. The Museum is a private collection of arrowheads, beads, pendants, and pottery of the Ancestral Puebloan cultures.

NATURAL BRIDGES NATIONAL MONUMENT, Lake Powell
In the 1200s, farmers from Mesa Verde migrated here, but by the 1300s the ancestral Puebloans migrated south. Later, Navajos and Paiutes lived here.

NEWSPAPER ROCK STATE HISTORIC MONUMENT, Blanding
The sandstone petroglyphs record 2,000 years of human activity in the area. The symbols represent Fremont, Ancestral Puebloan, Navajo and Anglo cultures.

UTAH FIELD HOUSE OF NATURAL HISTORY, Vernal
A state park and museum featuring exhibits in geology, paleontology, Indian prehistory, natural history, and a dinosaur garden.

UTAH MUSEUM OF NATURAL HISTORY, Salt Lake City
The Museum has a superb anthropology department, with over a half million pottery, basket, textile, and tool objects from Desert Archaic, Puebloan and Fremont cultures.

ZION NATIONAL PARK
Many ancestral cultures have been here. The Zion Human History Museum highlights the interaction of humans with the natural resources of Zion Canyon.

NEW MEXICO
AZTEC RUINS NATIONAL MONUMENT, Aztec
The largest ancestral Pueblo community in the Animas valley. The people of Aztec built several multi-story buildings called "great houses" and many smaller structures.

BANDELIER NATIONAL MONUMENT, Los Alamos
Several thousand ancestral Pueblo dwellings inhabited from the 1100s to mid-1600s are here. Some of the sites, are in Frijoles Canyon near the Visitor Center.

BLACKWATER DRAW MUSEUM, E. NEW MEXICO UNIVERSITY, Portales
Displays artifacts discovered at the nearby Blackwater Locality No. 1 Site. Artifacts and displays describe and interpret life at the site from Clovis times.

CHACO CULTURE NATIONAL HISTORIC PARK, Nageezi
Chaco Canyon was a major center of ancestral Puebloan culture between AD 850 and 1250. It was a hub of ceremony, trade, and administration for the area.

CORONADO STATE MONUMENT, Bernalillo
Includes partially reconstructed ruins of the ancient Pueblo of Kuaua. The original murals in the kiva are considered the finest example of pre-contact mural art in U.S.

EL MALPAIS NATIONAL MONUMENT, Grants
The Puebloan peoples of Acoma, Laguna,and Zuni, and the Ramah Navajo tribes continue their ancestral uses of El Malpais including gathering herbs, and medicines.

EL MORRO NATIONAL MONUMENT, Ramah
Ancestral Puebloans lived on top of El Morro over 700 years ago. The Monument protects over 2,000 inscriptions and petroglyphs, as well as Ancestral Puebloan ruins.

FOLSOM MUSEUM; Folsom
Located in the town for which the unique 10,000-year-old Folsom spear points are named. The museum offers evidence of Folsom Man's occupation.

GILA CLIFF DWELLINGS NATIONAL MONUMENT, Silver City
Gila Cliff Dwellings offer a glimpse of the lives of the people of the Mogollon culture who lived in the Gila Wilderness from the 1280s through the early 1300s.

INDIAN PUEBLO CULTURAL CENTER, Albuquerque
Owned and operated by the 19 Indian Pueblos of New Mexico. The Center showcases the history and accomplishments of the Pueblo people, from Pre-Columbian times.

JEMEZ STATE MONUMENT, Jemez Springs
The Monument protects a massive stone-walled church and *convento*. The San José de los Jémez Mission complex was constructed with Pueblo labor in the 1620s.

MUSEUM OF NEW MEXICO, Santa Fe
Encompasses four museums in Santa Fe and five state monuments. The Museum of Indian Arts and Culture, tells the history of the Native American people of the Southwest.

PECOS NATIONAL HISTORICAL PARK, Pecos
Pecos preserves 12,000 years of history including the ancient pueblo and two Spanish Colonial Missions.

PETROGLYPH NATIONAL MONUMENT,
Protects hundreds of archeological sites and an estimated 25,000 images carved by native peoples and early Spanish settlers.

RED ROCK MUSEUM, Gallup
The museum uses archaeological collections from the area to illustrate the prehistory of northwest New Mexico. Gallery exhibits change several times a year.

WHEELWRIGHT MUSEUM OF THE AMERICAN INDIAN, Santa Fe
The Museum hosts changing exhibitions of contemporary and historic Native American art with an emphasis on the Southwest.

THE PUEBLOS OF NEW MEXICO

ACOMA PUEBLO
Known as Sky City, the Pueblo was strategically built on top of a 357-foot mesa. Acomans claim that their village is the oldest continuously inhabited city in the U.S.

COCHITI PUEBLO
The people of Cochiti continue Pueblo traditions and cultural practices. Cochiti is well known for craftsmanship in making jewelry, storyteller pottery, and drums.

ISLETA PUEBLO
Comprised of two small communities Oraibi and Chicale and the main Pueblo Isleta. Summer dances, their September Fair and Christmas Festival are open to the public.

JEMEZ PUEBLO
Public access to the Pueblo is very limited. Visitors are welcome at the adjacent Walatowa Visitors Center.

LAGUNA PUEBLO
Consists of six villages; Encinal, Laguna, Mesita, Paguate, Paraje and Seama. All celebrate the Feast of St. Joseph. Hundreds of booths offer native arts and crafts.

NAMBE PUEBLO
At the base of the Sangre de Cristo Mountains, Nambé was established around the 1300s and served as a cultural and religious center for the ancestral Pueblo people.

PICURIS PUEBLO
Traditional ceremonies are celebrated at the Pueblo. Picuris pottery is unique as it is made from micaceous clay that produces a texture and a subtle glitter.

POJOAQUE PUEBLO
The Poeh Cultural Center features Pueblo art, hosts traditional Indian dances on weekends and preserves the traditional crafts of the Tewa-speaking pueblos.

SANDIA PUEBLO
Just north of Albuquerque, the Pueblo's Bien Mur Indian Market is one of the largest Native American stores in the Southwest, offering arts, crafts, moccasins and drums.

SAN FELIPE PUEBLO
The pueblo is known for its beautiful dancing, particularly for the Feast of St. Philip, May 1, when men, women and children participate in traditional Green Corn Dance.

SAN ILDEFONSO PUEBLO
The center of the Pueblo arts revival. The pueblo is known for black-on-black pottery with black matte designs, artisans' homes in the pueblo are open to the public.

SAN JUAN PUEBLO
San Juan is known for its redware pottery, weaving and painting. The Oke-Oweenge Crafts Cooperative exhibits the art of the eight northern pueblos.

SANTA ANA PUEBLO
The Pueblo is not open daily to the public but is open on several feast days. Their pottery and fine woven articles are available at the Pueblo's Ta-Ma-Ya Cooperative.

SANTA CLARA PUEBLO
Their ancestors lived in the nearby Puyé Cliff Dwellings along a Santa Clara Canyon cliff face. Visitors prize their redware, carved blackware, and polychrome pottery.

SANTO DOMINGO PUEBLO
The village people have a distinguished history of making fine jewelry. The Santo Domingos are great traders much like their Mesa Verde and Chaco Canyon ancestors.

TAOS PUEBLO
Well known for its adobe multistoried homes, Taos is the northernmost of all the pueblos. The Pueblo sits at the base of the highest mountains in New Mexico

TESUQUE PUEBLO
The pueblo has stood on its site since 1200. The Tesuque people are one of the most traditional of all New Mexico Pueblos in observing ceremonies and preserving culture.

ZIA PUEBLO
Birthplace of the ancient sun symbol of multiple stylized rays radiating in each of the four directions from a central sun; and inspiration for the New Mexico State flag.

ZUNI PUEBLO
Zuni cultural values are the focus of the A:shiwi A:wan Museum & Heritage Center. Needlepoint and inlay jewelry is the focus of the Pueblo of Zuni Arts & Crafts.

COLORADO

ANASAZI HERITAGE CENTER, Dolores
A Bureau of Land Management repository for nearly 3 million ancestral Puebloan artifacts. Nearby are the Dominguez and Escalante Ruins and Lowry Pueblo.

CROW CANYON ARCHEOLOGICAL CENTER, Cortez
Dedicated to understanding, teaching, and preserving the history of the ancient Pueblo Indians who inhabited the canyons and mesas of the American Southwest

DINOSAUR NATIONAL MONUMENT, Dinosaur
Rock art of the Fremont Indian culture is common along the canyon walls and testifies to the allure these canyons and rivers had for prehistoric peoples.

MESA VERDE NATIONAL PARK, Mesa Verde
A world-class archeological site, the park offers visitors a spectacular look into the lives of the Ancestral Pueblo people.

ARIZONA

THE AMERIND FOUNDATION, Dragoon
Archaeological research institute and museum devoted to the study, preservation, and interpretation of prehistoric Native American cultures.

ARIZONA STATE MUSEUM, Tucson
Located on the University of Arizona campus, the museum explores prehistoric and contemporary Indian cultures of Arizona

BESH-BA-GOWA ARCHAEOLOGICAL PARK, Globe
The Hohokam established a pithouse settlement here around 900. Later, around 1225, Salado Indians began constructing the pueblo that can be seen today.

CANYON DE CHELLY NATIONAL MONUMENT, Chinle
One of the longest continuously inhabited areas of North America. Canyon de Chelly's distinctive architecture, artifacts, and rock imagery are well preserved.

CASA GRANDE RUINS NATIONAL MONUMENT, Coolidge
One of the largest prehistoric structures ever built in North America. Preserves the story of the Hohokam, "those who are gone."

Coconino National Forest — STABILIZATION CLASS, ELDEN PUEBLO

ELDEN PUEBLO PROJECT; Flagstaff
A 60+ room pueblo of the Sinagua culture and a Hopi ancestral site. Evidence from pottery shards indicate the pueblo was originally occupied from about 1065–1275.

GILA PUEBLO, Globe
Occupied for about 200 years beginning in the early 1200s. The ruins and museum are open to the public.

GRAND CANYON NATIONAL PARK
Puebloan people were in this area from 200 B.C. to A.D. 1300. The Hopi people of Arizona and the Zuni of New Mexico believe they emerged from the canyon.

HEARD MUSEUM, Phoenix
A world-class museum, the Heard specializes in the anthropology of prehistoric Southwest Native Americans and their contemporary art.

MESA SOUTHWEST MUSEUM, Mesa
The Gallery holds a collection of *Art of the Ancient Americas*. Nearby, the Mesa Grande ruins consist of a Hohokam platform mound used 1000-1400.

MONTEZUMA CASTLE NATIONAL MONUMENT, Camp Verde
A five-story, 20-room dwelling served as a "high-rise building" for Sinagua Indians over 600 years ago. One of the best preserved cliff dwellings in North America.

MUSEUM OF NORTHERN ARIZONA, Flagstaff
An award-winning permanent exhibit, "Native Peoples of the Colorado Plateau," documents 12,000 years of human occupation in the Colorado Plateau Region.

NAVAJO NATIONAL MONUMENT, Tonalea
Preserves three of the most intact cliff dwellings of the ancestral puebloan people (Hisatsinom). Rangers guide tours of the Keet Seel and Betatakin cliff dwellings.

PETRIFIED FOREST NATIONAL PARK
Ancestral Puebloans lived here too. Agate House is an eight-room pueblo constructed of petrified wood. Puerco Pueblo is a one-story structure of more than 100 rooms.

PUEBLO GRANDE MUSEUM; Phoenix
A Hohokam site that includes dwellings, storage rooms, and a segment of the canals developed for irrigation. The museum itself has a large display of artifacts.

TUZIGOOT NATIONAL MONUMENT, Camp Verde
A Sinagua pueblo consisting of 110 rooms including second and third story structures. The first buildings were built around 1000. The Sinagua were farmers.

WALNUT CANYON NATIONAL MONUMENT, Flagstaff
Walk in the footsteps of the people that lived here over 900 years ago. The Sinagua occupied these single story cliff dwellings from about 1100 to 1250.

WESTERN ARCHEOLOGICAL AND CONSERVATION CENTER, Tucson
A repository holding ethnographic and archeological materials from the National Parks and Monuments of the Southwest

WUPATKI NATIONAL MONUMENT, Flagstaff
The Wupatki pueblo was built around 1100. Access to the visitor center is easy, however, the climb down to and up from the pueblo can be a challenge for some.